let's travel in

THAILAND

Edited by Darlene Geis

A TRAVEL PRESS BOOK

SECOND PRINTING

PICTURE ACKNOWLEDGMENTS

Twenty-eight of the color illustrations in this book were taken in Thailand by Ace Williams. Photographs 7, 24, 27 and 28 are by Ewing Krainin. For the black-and-white photographs we wish to thank the Royal Thai Embassy; AP (Wide World Photos); UPI (Acme Photos); Ernst Haas from Magnum; Diane Rawson and V. Bucher from Photo Researchers; Frank Howe from F.P.G.; Mullen from Monkmeyer; and Ace Williams. The map was made by Enrico Arno.

Library of Congress Catalog Card Number: 65-28201

CONTENTS

BANGKOK

Chao Phraya River

THONBURI

Rama IV Road

ANDAMAN

SEA

GULF of SIAM

MALAYA

Phet Buri 18

Nakhon Pathom 21

Bang-Pa-In 22

Bangkok 1–16

19

17

CAM

Locales of thirty-two full-page pictures

THAILAND, JEWEL OF THE EAST

THE ancient kingdom of Siam has become a modern nation, known today as Thailand (TIE-*land*), Land of the Free. The Thais, whose very name means "free," are indeed an independent people, for their country is one of the few in Asia that has never been a European colony. Thailand, in spite of some westernization, still retains the splendor of its glittering temples and bright palaces. And, deep in its jungles, there are ruins that tell of its fabled past.

This tropical country, whose national emblem is an elephant, is shaped, appropriately enough, like an elephant's head in profile. The long trunk curves about two-thirds of the way down the Malay Peninsula; the spreading elephant ear is surrounded by Laos (LAH-*ohss*) and Cambodia; the forehead pushes against Burma.

At the heart of Southeast Asia, Thailand, with its tradition of liberty, is the rallying point for those nations that oppose Communism. It is in Bangkok, the country's capital, that we find the headquarters of SEATO (Southeast Asia Treaty Organization) flying the flags of its member nations—Australia, France, Great Britain, New Zealand, Pakistan, the Philippines, Thailand and the United States.

The 200,000 square miles of Thailand may be divided into four sections. The narrow southern peninsula is the source of most of the country's tin and rubber, and its long shoreline arching around the Gulf of Siam is strung with fishing villages and balmy seaside resorts. The central plain is a broad, flat carpet of green on which nearly half of the 23,000,000 Thais live. The mighty river Chao Phraya (*chow prah-yah*) flows from north to south through the plain. Its numerous branches and a network of canals irrigate the rich rice fields and form a pattern of water roads, the chief transportation system of Thailand.

Northeast Thailand, with its poor soil and unreliable rainfall, raises little more than the rice needed for local consumption and devotes most of its land to livestock. The rest of the north is hilly and somewhat cooler. Here the great teak forests spread across the land, and ponderous elephants are put to work bulldozing, hoisting the heavy logs and hauling them to the river which will float the wood down to the Port of Bangkok.

9

LAND OF SMILES

Nature has smiled on Thailand, and the gentle Thais smile back. Their country is an Eastern Eden, a land of perpetual summertime where the living is easy. In this warm, moist climate, food—especially rice—is plentiful, and poverty brings little hardship. Because of the steamy heat, clothing is scanty for rich and poor alike, while the problem of shelter can be solved with the simplest thatched roof to keep out the rain. Numerous little canals, called *klongs,* afford nearly everyone an opportunity to bathe and wash frequently, though the water is far from clean.

People who live on the klongs of Thailand have running water right at their doorstep.

And the abundant fish swimming in the *klongs* are easy to catch and good to eat.

Nor do the Thais suffer from economic slavery. Nearly 90 per cent of the people are farmers, and most of them own the land they work. Freedom from want has made the Thais a cheerful and agreeable people, and their national religion, Buddhism, has also contributed to their attitude. For Buddhism instills in its followers a serene acceptance of life, and a relative disregard for the material objects that other peoples strive for so bitterly.

The inhabitants of this happy land are exceptionally attractive. The Thais are rather small, delicately boned, graceful and supple. A little darker than the Chinese, they have straight black hair and dark, almond-shaped eyes, and the women are among the most beautiful in the Orient. These handsome, fun-loving people are the ideal denizens of an Asiatic paradise.

THE STORY OF SIAM

Most Westerners know Siam for three things—a breed of blue-eyed cats; the famous Siamese twins, Chang and Eng; and a musical about an English governess at the court of a despotic Siamese king. The Siamese cat no longer exists in the country of its origin—the Thais will laughingly tell you that all the cats have gone to England, though it sometimes seems that they all went to the United States, where the Siamese twins lived out their days. And the musical, *The King and I*, which the

Thais feel presented an unjust portrait of one of their greatest monarchs, was banned from theaters in Thailand. So much for those meager scraps of information.

The actual history of Siam is fascinating. In earliest times all of the country south of China was inhabited by tribes that were split up into separate little kingdoms. The Thais had not yet arrived to lay claim to the land. They had founded their own independent kingdom in southern China and were a proud and free people even then, as their name signified. But in the thirteenth century the Mongol hordes of Kublai Khan (koo-*bligh* KAHN) came sweeping over China. Faced with oppression by this powerful new empire, the Thais chose to move southward instead.

They took over what is now northern Thailand, and built their first capital at Sukhothai (*sook-hoh*-TIE), which means "Happy Thai." This was a prophetic name, though for the next 400 years the young Siamese nation was involved in wars to gain more territory. As their country expanded, the Thais built new capitals, always moving southward. The old cities still stand, their ruined temples choked with jungle plants. They are markers, from north to south, of the Siamese nation's progress, leading to the most recent capital, Bangkok, which is only about one hundred and sixty years old.

THE FABULOUS SIAMESE KINGS

The ancient splendors of Siam reflected the glory of her great warrior-kings. From the thirteenth century on, Siam had a succession of remarkable rulers who wrested the rich land from its earlier settlers, and whose power was absolute. One of the first kings of Siam was Rama Kamheng (RAH-*mah kahm*-HANG), a military genius and a wise man, to boot. Day or night, any of Rama's subjects could strike the enormous bell in front of his palace gate, and the king himself would appear in all his magnificence to listen to their grievances and mete out justice. Rama borrowed the alphabet from the Cambodian tribes whom he had conquered, and it is the basis for the Thais' written language today.

Later kings waged war mounted on rare white elephants. The temples and palaces of their capital cities were dazzling, and the kings themselves were hedged around with ceremonies and edicts that made them almost godlike. The penalty was death for rocking the king's boat, death for touching a royal personage, death for whispering in the audience chamber, and subjects had to prostrate themselves before their king and crawl to him on hands and knees. Increasing contact with Europeans eventually toned down this excessive royal etiquette.

One king of the seventeenth century had a Greek advisor, at whose

suggestion he sent a glittering delegation to King Louis XIV of France. Even the lavish French court was impressed. In the 1860's King Mongkut (MOHNG-*koot*), also known as Rama IV, employed a Mrs. Anna Leonowens at his court. As he wrote, "She will be an English School mastress here and . . . it is not pleasant to us if the School mastress much morely endeavor to convert the scholars to Christianity than teaching language, literature, etc., etc. . . ." From this sample of the King's English it is easy to recognize the originals of *The King and I*.

TWENTIETH-CENTURY CHANGES

Rama IV's son came to the throne of Siam at the age of sixteen, and he continued his father's westernization of the country. It was Rama V who abolished slavery and the practice of groveling before the king. He was an enlightened ruler who realized the importance to Siam of being able to communicate with the European nations that she had been trading with for nearly 400 years.

Rama V established a school to teach English and sent Thai ambassadors to represent him in European countries. At the same time he imported foreign advisors to work with him in Bangkok. Many upper-class Thais began sending their sons to schools and universities in England at the turn of the century. By 1949 there were so many graduates of Eton, Harrow, Cambridge and Oxford in Siam that, according to one of the alumni, the country's new name could well be expanded to "Old-School-Tie-Land."

While her neighbors in Indochina, Burma and the Malay Peninsula had lost their national identities and become European colonies, Siam remained a self-governing nation which dealt on an equal footing with the countries of the West. In 1917 King Rama VI, who had gone to school in England and was an honorary British general, declared war against Germany and Austria-Hungary and sent Thai troops to join the fighting in France. The troops were actual Allies, not colonials.

But the influence of European schooling was eventually to have its repercussions in the monarchy itself. In 1932 a group of young intellectuals, fresh from the universities, returned to Thailand with the idea that their old-fashioned absolute monarchy should be modified by a constitution. They effected a mild sort of revolution, and Thailand has had more than 25 changes of government since. They have usually been accomplished gently, because bloodshed is abhorrent to the Buddhist Thais. Now the country is a constitutional monarchy. The king is the head of state, but the real power is in the hands of the prime minister.

During World War II, the Japanese occupied Siam and forced her to declare war on the Allies. A Free Thai resistance movement grew both inside and outside the country, and many students who had been studying abroad when the war broke out were parachuted into Siam with British and American agents. At war's end the country joined the United Nations, and Bangkok has become the Asiatic headquarters for a number of United Nations agencies. Bangkok's airport is one of the busiest and most modern in that part of the world, located at the crossroads of many major air routes of Asia. New York, home of the U.N., is almost exactly halfway around the world from Bangkok. As a consequence, the capital of Thailand is an ideal meeting place for East and West.

BANGKOK, THE VENICE OF THE EAST

Thailand's capital is uniquely beautiful. Situated on the winding Chao Phraya River about 20 miles from the Gulf of Siam, the sprawling city is crisscrossed with hundreds of canals, or *klongs*. The traffic on these crowded waterways is a picturesque conglomeration of paddle boats, motor launches, houseboats, and sampans—the shallow Chinese skiffs that dart in and out among the larger craft. Houses line the water's edge, some of them built on stilts overhanging the *klongs*, or even on floats. And there are communities of water dwellers, who live permanently aboard their sampans, bathing in the city canals and drinking the muddy water, apparently immune to any germs it may carry.

Bangkok means "water-flower village," but the city has far outgrown its original poetic name. It spreads over an enormous flat area like a cluster of small villages tied together by the river and canals. The Thais' name for their capital is Krung Thep (KROONG TAPE), or "City of Angels," and many of the country people know it only by that name. Including its suburbs, Bangkok has nearly 2,000,000 inhabitants, and is the largest city in Southeast Asia. The old capital of Thonburi (*tohn-boo-*REE), on the west bank of the river, is now a suburb of Bangkok.

Bangkok today is a thriving metropolis with broad boulevards and bright new buildings, many of them air-conditioned for comfort in the muggy tropical heat. In the tree-shaded residential sections, brilliant flower gardens surround the houses and verandahs. And, matching the

13

klongs for fascination, there are the narrow alleys and old back streets teeming with Bangkok's large Chinese population. Here we will find hundreds of tiny shops and stalls heaped with goods from the far corners of the world. Sapphires, ivory, jade, precious silks, snakeskin and crocodile leather goods, incense, candles, birds, strange and wonderful foods—all are displayed to the milling throngs.

Still, Bangkok would be a fairly typical Oriental city if it were not for the 400 temples that stud the town like flashing gems. Their glittering spires and brilliant tile roofs catch the sun, and transform a busy city into an exotic wonderland. Thailand's smiling people offer the visitor warmth and hospitality, and with their exotic temples they bestow on us the ultimate gift—the enchantment of faraway places.

The everyday life of Bangkok takes place against a backdrop of glittering temples.

Let's travel in

THAILAND

TEMPLE OF DAWN: ARCHITECTURAL FANTASY

NO OTHER place on earth has buildings that are as gay and fanciful as the wats (WAHTZ), or Buddhist temples, of Thailand. And in Bangkok, where nearly one-fifth of the city is occupied by these colorful edifices, the visitor soon falls under their bright spell. You can see that the wats are the artistic expression of a joyous and daring people.

This lovely Thai girl is sitting in front of Wat Arun (*ah*-ROON), the Temple of Dawn, and her delicate beauty contrasts with the fierce guardian demon towering behind her. The Temple of Dawn is the oldest one in Bangkok and it stands at the river's edge, its central *prang*, or tower, reaching nearly 250 feet into the sky. Four smaller *prangs* surround it, and there are a number of other sacred buildings on the grounds, including the well guarded temple in this picture.

Wat Arun is made of plaster spread over brick—the most ordinary building materials obtainable. But the Thais created something extraordinary here. Embedded in the plaster are bits and pieces of broken cups and saucers, and the colored fragments of pottery give the towers a jewel-encrusted look. When you see them from a distance glinting in the brilliant sun, or at night gleaming mysteriously in the moonlight, the towers of Wat Arun stagger the imagination.

The great storyteller W. Somerset Maugham spent some time across the river from Wat Arun at the old Oriental Hotel, and he wrote several stories set in Siam. In one of them he says this about the wats of Bangkok: "It makes you laugh with delight to think that anything so fantastic could exist on this somber earth. The artists who developed them step by step . . . had the courage to pursue their fantasy to the limit." The Thais' originality creates new and delightful surprises in every temple.

16

OLD CHINESE FIGURE: TEMPLE ORNAMENT

HERE, we are looking at one of the oldest parts of the Temple of Dawn. In Thailand these ornate buildings grow shabby in a short time, for the hot and humid climate soon rots their beams, and the plaster crumbles away from the brickwork. Rather than keep the old temples in good repair, the Thais prefer to build new additions to them. Their Buddhist religion teaches them to "make merit," to do good deeds that will be credited to their account in the next life, and one of the highest-scoring ways of making merit is to build a wat. Consequently the country blossoms with temples—there are 19,000 of them in Thailand—representing a prodigious amount of merit stored up over the years. But none of the buildings endure for long.

The grounds and gateways of many Thai wats and palaces are decorated with stone figures that are decidedly Chinese in origin. The venerable Chinese gentleman being admired by the little girl is typical. Thousands of these stone images were brought to Thailand long ago in trading vessels. Thai ships went to China loaded with goods, but would have had to return with too light a cargo, and the Chinese obligingly supplied them with grotesque stone carvings which were used for ballast. The Thais, whose native sculptors tended to specialize in statues of Buddha, found the assorted Chinese works were a fine addition to their temples and palaces.

Ancient Chinese statues, a long way from home, are smiling guardians of Thailand's ornate buildings.

18

FLOATING MARKET: THE WATER PEOPLE

BANGKOK'S waterways teem with the colorful life of the city, and nearly half of its population lives on the crowded *klongs*. Some of these canals are highways, others are floating markets where all the varied merchandise of a bazaar is heaped up in hundreds of little boats. And some *klongs* are palm-fringed avenues where colonies of sampans are moored, housing the water people who spend their entire lives afloat.

Along the banks of the *klongs*, flimsy houses raised on stilts lean against shops with open fronts. In the early morning, boats come floating down from the country loaded with melons, coconuts and vegetables, and the *klongs* are noisy with the singsong cries of the vendors. Some of the boats are equipped with stoves, and the smells of fried fish, garlic and spices fill the warm air. Motor launches thread their precarious way through the maze of boat traffic, carrying tourists through this unbelievable water city.

Sixty years ago, Bangkok had only one road, and people had to travel by boat on the rivers. When new roads were constructed, they were raised above the low land on banks, so that they would not be flooded during the wet season. The digging necessary for building the banks left ditches alongside the roads, and in time the ditches filled with water and became the busy *klongs* that add their rich life to the fascination of Bangkok.

The *klongs* have many uses. Some of the poorer people even find their food in the soupy *klong* water. Edible vegetation floats in some places on the surface of the muddy-looking canals. In other spots, green, spinach-like plants are cultivated in floating gardens anchored by poles. And fish dart through the murky water in abundance. Children catch them easily with lines, and after a morning's sport they return home with lunch for the whole family. *Klong* life, so different from anything we know in our cities, has something to recommend it.

RIVER
FESTIVAL:
TIME OF JOY

THAILAND'S winding rivers and canals, that play so large a part in the people's lives, figure in their festivals, too. One of the loveliest celebrations takes place in October or November, usually on the night of the full moon. At this season the weather is fair and cool after the period of rains. The long, hard months of plowing and planting rice are past, the Buddhist Lent is over, and it is a time of rejoicing and celebration.

In our picture we see a group of girls preparing for the *Loy Krathong* (*loy kraht-*HOHN), which means "to float a leaf cup." For this festival everyone has a *krathong*, usually in the shape of a leaf or flower cup, although some are more fancifully decorated to look like birds, boats, snakes, or even miniature temples. Each cup holds a candle and some incense sticks, and occasionally a small coin is added for good measure.

When the full moon rises, people all over the land light the candles and incense in their *krathongs*, and set them afloat on river and canal. Hundreds of thousands of these little lights bob along the waterways of Thailand, as onlookers watch from boats and from the shore. The flickering *krathongs* are thought to symbolize the floating away of sins and troubles as they drift out of sight. The people turn away from the moon-washed river and walk home with lighter hearts.

Most Thai festivals, whether national or religious, are characterized by gaiety and merriment. Each month there is at least one big celebration, where the participants wear their best clothes and carry bright flowers and incense. Frequently there are colorful processions on the roads and—most spectacular of all—along the rivers and canals. Even the more solemn rites are designed to make people feel happier, and when worshipers gather at their temples to listen to readings from the Buddhist scriptures, the glittering buildings must add a lift to the spirit. The same is true of the royal palaces, whose bright colors and fantastic shapes are gay rather than pompous.

THE GRAND PALACE: ROYAL RESIDENCE

THE splendor of the old Siamese court has been kept intact within the walled enclosure of the Grand Palace. This magnificent group of buildings and their paved courtyards cover an area almost a mile square. And above the white walls the intricate towers, spires and peaked roofs can be seen from the streets of Bangkok, hinting at the fairyland within.

In 1782 the Siamese king, whose capital lay across the river at Thonburi, became insane and was executed. After the royal execution, the people elected General Chakkri (DJAHK-*kree*) their new king, and he became Rama I, founder of the present dynasty. Rama I built his palace in the new capital of Bangkok, where he surrounded himself with all the lavish trappings of an Oriental potentate.

In this picture we are standing just outside the Chakkri Hall, one of the more recent additions to the palace. Built according to the plans of a British architect, the Chakkri Hall disguises its European design under roofs that are unmistakably Siamese. The many-tiered roofs of tile are insulation against the heat, and their steeply pitched sides allow rain to run off quickly. In suiting their architecture to the climate, the Thais have developed a style that is both striking and distinctive.

Amid the splendors of the Grand Palace the young queen and her children play a game without protocol.

PALACE COURTYARD: OUTSIDE THE CHAPEL ROYAL

THE flamboyant ritual that surrounds the king of Thailand takes place against this background of elaborate buildings. Here is the very heart of the kingdom, where ancient ceremonials are re-enacted to bring Siam's gaudy past to life again. Behind the gilded demigod—half man, half bird—is the Chapel Royal, known as the Temple of the Emerald Buddha. It is the king's own place of worship, and within the temple one of Thailand's most sacred relics is enshrined.

The Emerald Buddha was carved from a single piece of green translucent jasper and stands about 31 inches high. It was made centuries ago, probably by a Greek convert to Buddhism in northwest India, and eventually it found its way to Siam. The revered image is robed in garments of gold and precious gems, and its gorgeous vestments are changed each season by the king himself. The future of the Chakkri dynasty and the destiny of Thailand are believed to depend upon the Emerald Buddha.

Royal pageantry from another age still surrounds Thailand's modern king.

Every May, on the evening of the full moon, this courtyard is the scene of a great Buddhist festival. Monks and laymen chant poems in praise of Buddha, while the King and Queen lead a candlelit procession three times around the temple. As they move solemnly between the buildings, hundreds of little bells hanging under the eaves tinkle in the evening breeze.

26

CLASSICAL
DANCER:
ELABORATE
MAKE-BELIEVE

THE glittering architectural style of Siamese temples is repeated in the spiked head-dress and jewel-encrusted costume of this young dancer. Many of the Thai arts came from India, and the lavish use of color and ornament are common to both countries. Thai classical dancing stems directly from the Indian dance, and this girl is dressed to play a part in an old Indian legend. She will use her fingers, hands, head and eyes in a complicated language of gesture which her Thai audience understands completely.

For example, when the dancer puts a hand on her heart, that means love; if she stamps her foot and points with her forefinger, she is indicating anger; when she raises a finger to her mouth, she is smiling; and when she bends her pretty head and touches her forehead, the audience knows it must grieve with her, for she is expressing sorrow. The dance gestures are intricate, and they demand such remarkable flexibility that performers must start studying at an early age to perfect themselves in this demanding art.

The carefree people of Thailand are devoted to their music and dancing. There are special theaters in the cities where everyone—from ricksha coolie to wealthy noble—sits enthralled for a four-hour performance. In country villages, traveling troupes unpack their fabulous costumes and dance in the temple courtyard to celebrate a holiday, a fair, or the birthday of a rich patron.

As the musicians weave their odd melodies with flutes, gongs, xylophones and drums, the dancers sway, matching their movements to the sinuous music. Their costumes twinkle, and the stiff fabrics disguise the living bodies beneath them. Watching a Thai dancer perform in a temple courtyard, you have the impression that a part of the building has come to life and is expressing the joyous feelings of the people who created it.

WORKSHOP
IN BANGKOK:
BUILDING
SPIRIT HOUSES

THE glorious temples of Thailand are all dedicated to Buddha, the founder of the Thais' religion. But long before Buddhism was brought here from India, the primitive tribes who inhabited the country believed in spirits. That belief still persists, and spirits, most of them evil, are still thought to be abroad in the land.

When a Thai family builds a new residence, there is always the possibility that it has disturbed the spirits who live on the property. In order to protect their new home from retaliatory harm or mischief, the family puts up a little model house on a pole for the spirits to live in. This spirit house must be located somewhere on the grounds where the shadow of the human dwelling will never fall on it.

Offerings of incense, fruit, flowers and rice are left in the little house on the pole, because the spirits must be kept happy at all costs. Strangely enough, though they resemble bird houses and are temptingly stocked with food, the spirit houses are almost never occupied by birds. Perhaps even the birds of Thailand respect these invisible beings.

Thailand's roads are still rather primitive. You can always tell that a certain curve or corner is especially treacherous, because there will be a small grove of spirit houses planted there by hopeful drivers. Their theory is that if the malignant spirits who haunt the place are given an attractive home they will not spitefully endanger the drivers who must pass this way. At the very least, the colorful houses are an effective warning to motorists to drive carefully.

Even sophisticated city-dwellers use spirit houses, and in Bangkok there are several small factories that turn them out in every size, shape and color. As you can see, they are a great deal more cheerful than our idea of a haunted house.

30

NEW ERAWAN HOTEL: OUTDOOR SHRINE

AS BEFITS the largest, most modern hotel in Bangkok, the Erawan (*eh-rah*-VAHN) Hotel has a large, modern spirit house with all the trimmings. In this picture we see a Thai girl, dressed in the wonderful silk for which her country is famous, making an offering of joss sticks. The joss stick originated in China, and is an especially pleasant form of incense. It is simply a reed coated with a paste made from sweet-smelling woods, and the girl places it in a bowl of sand where it burns like a stick of punk.

The spirits who were dispossessed when this hotel was built are well looked after. The ropes of bright flowers hung around the spirit house are a common decoration in Thailand, where flowers grow in tropical profusion. Instead of arranging the blossoms in bouquets or wreaths, the Thais take the petals apart and string them in colorful patterns, so that they no longer resemble the original flowers. Sometimes the gar-lands are painted, to disguise the different blooms still more. The incense, flowers and other offerings are lavish enough to keep even the fussiest spirits happy, and they are insurance that the service at the hotel will not be disrupted by supernatural high jinks.

Most of Bangkok's hotels are air-conditioned, and because the city has been the site for international conferences, it is one of the few places in the Orient that combine an exotic background with all the comforts of home.

The crowded streets of Bangkok are the crossroads of East and West.

HOLIDAY IN
THE TROPICS:
A CHANCE TO
COOL OFF

BANGKOK is an exciting city for tourists because of its blend of cosmopolitan pleasures and fascinating sights. The city, which is only six feet above sea level, is always hot, even in the coolest months of January, February and early March. But foreigners can enjoy the luxury of air-conditioned hotels, and a refreshing swim in the cool, clear waters of the Erawan pool. Here, shut away from the noise, the color and the teeming life of Bangkok, visitors can renew themselves for their next bout of sight-seeing.

This new hotel and many of the more recent public buildings in the city are painted a plain, creamy white, and their surfaces are smooth and unadorned. They are a welcome rest for eyes surfeited with the bright colors and intricate patterns of Bangkok's temples and palaces.

Foreigners, or "*farangs*" (*fah*-RAHNKS) as they are known in Thailand, do their swimming in a pool. But the Thais manage to bathe several times a day in their country's numerous *klongs*. Poorer families bathe in the crowded *klongs* wearing yesterday's clothes, which get laundered at the same time. Indoor bathing facilities are unique in Thailand. The large modern hotels have plumbing, of course, and it works fairly well—if the hotel spirits have been properly appeased. But in smaller hotels and nearly all houses, there is a different arrangement. A large jar of water stands in the bathroom with a dipper next to it. The bather sloshes cold water over himself with the dipper, and it drains away through cracks in the floor. This is a delightful way to cool off in a country where water is often the only defense against the wilting heat. Water is so important to the Thais that they have superstitiously decorated many of their buildings with figures of serpents called Nagas (NAH-*guhz*). The Nagas are demigods believed to be the givers of rain, and you can see modernized versions of them near the hotel swimming pool, gloating at the sight of so much water.

34

THE MARBLE TEMPLE: GIFT OF A KING

SIAMESE kings have a custom of building new temples to replace old ones decayed by time or destroyed by war. Usually they have added fine new buildings to existing wats, but King Rama V decided instead to build one completely new temple and to make it the most splendid and lasting one in his realm. This famous king, also known as Chulalongkorn (*choo-*LAH-*long-korn*), was the Siamese prince who was taught by Anna Leonowens, and he introduced Siam to many modern Western ways. In the Marble Temple he had his architects adapt the ancient Siamese designs to white marble imported from Italy. The result, as you can see, is magnificent, and the temple looks as fresh and new as it did more than 60 years ago, when it was built.

The roof of Chinese tile is decorated with the golden serpents called Nagas. According to Thai mythology, each year's rainfall depends upon the number of Nagas who are responsible for it, but the fewer the better. If many of these serpents are assigned to look after the rainfall, each one is inclined to let the other fellow do it, with the result that no one does anything and there is a drought. But if a single Naga has to shoulder the responsibility, it makes for a good wet year. The Nagas in our picture have evidently been on the job, and we see the Marble Temple and its courtyard gleaming in the sunshine after a sudden tropical shower.

Siamese schoolgirls kneel at prayers in a ruined temple built a thousand years ago.

GOLDEN
BUDDHA:
TRANQUILLITY

THE artistry of the Thais is expressed not only in their religious buildings but also in the statues of Buddha that adorn them. Although the buildings are generally not made of very durable materials, the statues, many of them cast in bronze, have lasted through the centuries, serene and unchanged. Some of the bronze Buddhas date from the fourteenth century, when the influence of Greek sculptors filtered into Southeast Asia from the West. The Greeks under Alexander the Great had invaded Persia and India a thousand years earlier, and eventually their art, and the Chinese craft of casting in bronze, met and blended in Thai sculpture.

There are very strict rules imposed upon the artist who portrays Buddha. The great teacher must be shown only in one of four prescribed attitudes—standing, walking, sitting or reclining. A standing Buddha is teaching; the seated statues mean different things depending upon the position of the hands. The Buddha in our picture is seated in the classic attitude of meditation, cross-legged with his hands resting tranquilly in his lap.

Although Buddha is venerated as a man, and not worshiped as a god, his images are always stylized rather than realistic. When we look at his statues, we do not see a portrait of a human being, but rather the personification of an ideal. The earliest and most authentic portraits have been carefully copied, then the copies were copied, and by this time there is very little individual variation in the statues. Now tradition dictates precisely what Buddha must look like. His eyebrows must be precisely arched, his nose must resemble a parrot's beak, and his chin is supposed to look like a mango stone. Beyond these restrictions the statues may be made in any size, from miniatures to the reclining colossus in Wat Po, which is over 100 feet long. They may be gilded, jeweled or inlaid with mother-of-pearl, but their message is always the same—tranquillity through contemplation.

38

THAI CRAFTSMAN: MAKING LACQUERED TABLES

NO MATTER how humble a Thai house is, it nearly always contains a statue of Buddha. If there is no other furniture, the statue is set on a shelf. But whenever possible, Buddha's image rests in a place of honor on a lacquered table like the one the young man is finishing in this picture. Thai lacquer work was once very popular all over the Orient, and there was a brisk export trade in it. Some of the fine old pieces remain today in the National Museum in Bangkok and in palaces and temples. But the painstaking old methods, learned from the Chinese, are fast disappearing.

The modern practitioners of lacquer work use bright colors and produce their work in quantity. Since lacquer dries best in a humid climate, a backyard in Bangkok, like this one, offers ideal conditions for the craft. Perhaps the best known of the Siamese minor arts is their nielloware (NYEHL-*loh-ware*). The craftsman etches an elaborate design on silver- or gold-plated metal and then fills it in with a black alloy. The crowded shopping sections of Bangkok offer these and many other Siamese specialties for sale. When you walk through the market quarters and peer into the stalls and curio shops, practically all the faces you see are Chinese. Then you realize that although the merchandise has been made by the Siamese, it is the large and energetic Chinese population that has taken over commerce and retail trade.

Bowls of hammered brass are turned out by hand in this country of fine craftsmen.

BANGKOK
SHOW PLACE:
NATIVE
ELEGANCE

THE Thais are not a commerce-minded people, and frequently they leave it to outsiders to put their beautiful native handicrafts on a paying basis. One of the most successful businessmen in Bangkok is an American named James Thompson, managing director of the Thai Silk Company. He came to Thailand about 15 years ago, fell in love with the country and its culture, and decided to stay. Thompson took the native art of silk weaving and organized it into an industry, and now the vivid and luxurious Thai silks make bright splashes of color in many countries of the world.

Jim Thompson lives on a *klong* in Bangkok, where he recently built himself a Thai house by putting together a group of old buildings made of hand-carved teak. Complete even to a spirit house in the garden, this remarkable home with its soaring roofs and cool high-ceilinged rooms has become a new landmark in Bangkok. The beautifully detailed interior is a perfect background for the delicate Thai girl who is modeling a gown made of rich, creamy Thai silk.

It proved to be almost impossible to find modern builders who knew how to make the fine old Siamese houses. In the past 30 years the vogue has been for copies of English Tudor or Victorian mansions and American split-level ranch houses. Only in the poorer sections of Bangkok do the steep-roofed wooden houses of old Siam still exist. Thompson went to some of his silk weavers and offered to buy their old houses for enough money to enable them to build modern Western homes. And that is how he got the lovely old buildings that make this striking example of ancient Siamese architecture. Now it is opened twice a week for guided tours, and the proceeds go to the School for the Blind in Bangkok.

MOTHER
AND CHILD:
PAINTING
UMBRELLAS

THE contrast between wealth and poverty in Thailand is softened by the easygoing and cheerful nature of the people. Even the poorest of them have enough to eat, and their attitude toward work is pleasant and relaxed. There is always time for a chat, and young children need not be separated from their parents in the course of a working day. Many children pitch in and help, especially on the farms, and jobs are not done at the frantic, driving tempo that can rob them of all pleasure. This woman, painting designs on umbrellas while her little girl stands by, is a far cry from the harried factory worker whose child must be left in a nursery. The Buddhist philosophy sets no value on material possessions, and consequently the Thais live happily with very little.

These gentle, loving people are especially fond of children, and as a result the small fry encountered in Thailand are delightful. Parents are affectionate, and they teach their children manners at a very early age. You will see even the tiniest boys and girls greeting their father with special Thai decorum. They press their palms together, fingers pointed upward, and hands raised well above the forehead as a mark of respect. The children are taught by example the Thai virtues of kindliness and generosity and—as we can see in this picture—monumental patience.

While mother cuts sugar cane, her little boy plays soldier with a long stalk.

45

FIGHTING KITE: NATIONAL PASTIME

ALTHOUGH the Thais are peaceable and good-natured, they can be fierce and violent when aroused. This more aggressive side of their nature is seldom seen in daily life, but it is reflected in their curious sports and games, nearly all of which involve some form of combat. Kite flying, which most of us think of as a simple childhood pastime, becomes a highly skilled form of aerial battle with the Thais.

From February to April, when the monsoon blows over the land, the wind-swept skies are alive with kites. Siamese kites have genders. There is the male kite, large and star-shaped, like the one in this picture. It is called a *chula* (*choo*-LAH), and it has barbs with which it attempts to cut the line of the female kite called a *pakpao* (*pahk*-PAH-*oh*). The *pakpao* is smaller and has a long tail. It tries to snarl up the line of the larger kite and bring it to earth. When the winds are strong and the Thais' fighting spirit is aroused, they throng to parks and fields to bet on the outcome of the kite fights.

Thai boxing is a vicious sport, a no-holds-barred contest in which elbows, knees and feet are brought freely into play. Prayers are said at the beginning of each bout, and music is played during the Donnybrook, but these gentle trimmings do not lessen the violence. The Thais have their own form of bullfighting too, where bull is pitted against bull. This idea of matching animals against one another in mortal combat is a favorite one of the Thais. They have fighting crickets and—most popular of all—fighting fish. Originally found in the *klongs,* the fish are now bred for courage as well as beauty. Two males, brilliantly colored and with broad graceful fins, are put into one tank. They make a brave display, fluttering their fins and looking as belligerent as it is possible for a fish to look. Then they swim in to the attack, biting or nibbling one another until one fish either dies or gives up.

ROADSIDE SCENE: POLE NET FISHERMEN

SIAMESE fighting fish may be popular pets, but other varieties of fish constitute the mainstay of the Thai diet. In the shallow waters of the Gulf of Siam, commercial fishermen set huge traps made of woven bamboo stakes, in which they catch everything from tuna to anchovies. Oysters and other mollusks conveniently attach themselves to long poles lowered into the Gulf. When the poles are thickly encrusted, they are pulled up and the shellfish are picked off like ripe fruit.

Thai ingenuity goes far beyond fishing with a rod and line. The flat inland country with its shallow waterways and flooded rice fields is a perpetual harvest land of fish, and there are many ways to catch them. Sometimes you see the Thai farmers wading out into the muddy water to work their long bamboo-pole nets. They raise the pole until the net is lowered into the water. Then after a short interval they pull the pole down like a pump handle, the bulging net comes up, and usually there is a flash of silver as the smaller fish flop around.

Often a line of men walk slowly through the water, herding a group of fish before them. Then they reach down and catch the slippery flopping creatures with bare hands, or spear them with a sharp stick. No matter how they are caught, the fish are always served with rice, the Thais' staple food.

Thai boxing is a far more rugged sport than the Marquis of Queensberry ever dreamed of.

49

OUTDOOR MARKET: EXOTIC FOODS

THE Thai people enjoy a deliciously varied cuisine, and in this picture we can see the lavish harvest of native foods spread out temptingly. The art of preparing food in this hot and humid country is aimed at enticing and stimulating appetites dulled by the oppressive heat. The Thais have succeeded so well that eating has become a favorite pastime, and outdoor food stalls do a thriving business. The sociable Thais stop for a bite to eat with one another at frequent intervals during the day.

The basic food is rice, and if you are invited for a meal, the phrase is, "Come and eat rice." "With the rice" covers a multitude of other foods—fish, lobster, prawns, tiny pinhead crabs, ants' eggs, banana-tree flowers,

At an outdoor market the buying of vegetables can be a serious transaction.

fowl and pork. These are prepared with exotic spices and herbs, and the dishes are planned to have contrast of texture and flavor and a variety of colors and shapes. The fruits of Thailand are worthy of Eden. Each season brings its own beautifully scented and colored fruit. Mangoes, at least a dozen kinds of bananas, litchis (LEE-*chihs*), pineapples and palm fruit add their cool, sweet refreshment to the spicy Thai fare.

50

BUDDHIST MONKS: BEGGING FOR BREAKFAST

EVERY morning, shortly after sunrise, you can see a strange sight in this land that knows no hunger. From every temple, in villages and cities, the saffron-robed monks emerge, carrying their begging bowls. With shaved heads and bare feet they move silently from house to house, holding out their bowls for a bit of food. Each householder puts some morsel of rice or fish or vegetable in the bowl, and then thanks the monk for the privilege of being his benefactor and thus making merit. The monk does not reply. He, too, knows that it is more blessed to give than to receive.

There are more than 300,000 monks in Thailand, although only about a third of that number are permanent members of the sangha (SOONG-*gah*), or brotherhood. The others are novices and student-assistants whose term of monkhood varies from a few days to several years. Nearly every young man in Thailand spends some time as a monk, and even the present king was a member of the sangha for three weeks. After a cheerful ordination service the novice, his head shaved, and garbed in the bright yellow of the Buddhists, takes up residence in a dormitory building of the temple compound. His only possessions are a razor, an umbrella, and a small cloth through which he strains any liquid he drinks. This is done to safeguard him from inadvertently swallowing (and therefore killing) a live insect—for taking life, even accidentally, is against Buddhist principles. Nevertheless, the Thai Buddhists do eat meat and fish. If they do not kill an animal themselves, eating its flesh is no sin.

Monks may not handle money, and they must accept their food from the community at large. Their strict monastic discipline is sharply at variance with the easygoing merriment of Thai life. But the serious young men we see in this picture will return to their homes one day, spiritually enriched by this period of study, meditation and denial spent in their Buddhist wat.

RELIGIOUS GIFTS: FESTIVE DONATIONS

THE Thais practice the art of giving with a loving attention to detail. Their gifts, however humble, are always beautifully presented, and this is especially true of donations brought to the monks on certain religious holidays. The decorative wrappings express the glad and generous spirit of the giver. The shop in this picture specializes in appropriate presents for members of the sangha, as well as the colorful altar decorations brought to the wats by grateful parishioners.

The Buddhist Lent is observed from July to October, a period that coincides with the rainy season between the sowing and harvesting of crops. Consequently this is the most popular time for young men to become temporary members of the sangha. Gifts, such as the ones we see here, are brought to the wats by families of the novices, and the ordination ceremonies are brightened by these gaily colored presents.

Young men give precious days of their youth to temple service— the greatest gift of all.

During the entire Lenten period the faithful make frequent visits to the wats, bearing gifts—soap, tea, a saffron-yellow robe, a bowl. When the Lenten season is over, there is a great festival when friends exchange gifts of sweets. They also exchange the Four Blessings, which are tinged with typical Thai practicality: "May you live to an old age; may your face look youthful; may you have much happiness and good health."

54

TEMPLE SPIRE: HISTORIC MONUMENT

BUDDHISM took root in this country centuries before the Thais moved down from China. Here, in Nakhon Pathom (*nah*-KOHN *pat*-HOHM), about 27 miles west of Bangkok, is the oldest *chedi* (*cheh*-DEE), or bell-shaped tower, in Thailand, believed to date from the second century. This *chedi* contains relics of the original Buddha, brought from India in those distant days. The ancient temple was restored many times during its long history, and finally, in the last century, King Mongkut ordered the jungle cleared away from the ruins and encased the historic building in the glazed-tile structure we see here.

The Phra Pathom Chedi (*prah pat*-HOHM *cheh*-DEE) is one of the holiest places in Thailand, and the ashes of King Rama VI, who died in 1925, are enshrined beneath the golden Buddha standing at the entrance to the chapel. Whenever the reigning king of Thailand passes Phra Pathom, he must stop and make the traditional offering of candles and joss sticks here.

The legends surrounding the earliest tower hint at its kingly origin long ago. The story of Phra Pathom has a curious similarity to the ancient Greek myth of Oedipus, and encountering it in this faraway place is as strange as the discovery of the temple itself hidden in the jungle. An old chronicle tells of a tribal king who was warned by astrologers that his son would grow up to kill him. The little boy was abandoned and left to die, but his nurse took pity on the child and raised him in secrecy. When the boy grew up he became a great hero and killed the tyrannical ruler who was oppressing his people. The young man then became king, but when he discovered that it was his own father he had killed, he blamed his nurse, and put her to death too. Then, as an act of contrition, he built a tall *chedi* with a tower "as high as the wild pigeon flies." The monuments of bygone kings and queens are fascinating footnotes to Siamese history.

PAVILION IN
THE LAKE:
ROYAL SUMMER
PALACE

THIS lacelike Siamese pavilion, rising on stilts in the center of a little lake, is the Taj Mahal of Thailand. It was built on the grounds of the old Summer Palace by King Rama V (Chulalongkorn), as a memorial to his queen. That unfortunate lady was being rowed on the river in one of the magnificently gilded royal barges when it collided with another boat. The barge capsized, and the queen was left to struggle in the water while her horrified courtiers and the boatmen looked on but could do nothing to save her. The Siamese law making it a capital offense for anyone to touch a royal person was, in effect, a death sentence for the queen.

The Royal Summer Palace, now seldom used, is in Bang-Pa-In (*bahng-pah-INN*), about 36 miles north of Bangkok on the Chao Phraya River and not far from the ancient capital of Ayudhya (*ah-YOOT-tah-yah*). The main palace was built in the French style during the nineteenth century, when European influence at the court was strong. But when the bereaved king built this memorial to his wife, he chose pure Siamese architecture, and the graceful pillars and peaked roofs reflected in the lake are a perfect example of this style at its loveliest. Thailand erected a copy of the pavilion at the Paris International Exhibition in 1937, and in the twentieth century the influence of Siamese art was at last felt in Europe.

Stately gilded barges used to carry royalty on the rivers. Now they have been replaced with less romantic launches.

58

SACRED CAVERN: SUBTERRANEAN BUDDHAS

N O ARCHITECT, however gifted, could hope to build a temple as mysterious and awesome as this cave. With the sunlight filtering down through an opening in the earth's surface, the underground chamber glows in a tawny light, and the images seem to have sprung from the very rock. These are the famous caves of Tham Khao Luang (*tahm* KAH-*oo* LOO-*ahng*), just outside of Phet Buri (*pet boo*-REE).

Phet Buri is a thriving city near the west coast of the Gulf of Siam. Its streets are crowded with bicycles and *samlors*—three-wheeled rickshas which are pedaled instead of pulled—and its shops are a colorful hodgepodge of Oriental merchandise. One of the best roads in Thailand —and at best they are none too good—runs from Bangkok through Phet Buri, and down the long, narrow elephant's trunk of land to Malaya. But if you travel off the road a few miles from Phet Buri, you come to these remarkable caverns, so remote in time and place from our modern lives.

Steps hewn out of rock lead down into the cave. Stalactites, like stony icicles, hang high above, and stalagmites thrusting up from the floor serve as pedestals for statues of the Buddha. White-robed Buddhist nuns sit on a bench in the first chamber, selling joss sticks and little squares of gold leaf to the devout. The patches of gold are placed on the larger images to repair the gilded surfaces. As you can see in this picture, they give the statues a sequinned look. Areas that are easier to reach—the hands and arms—are more heavily covered with gold than other parts. The cool, dim cavern is a pleasant place to spend some time, out of the brassy heat and glare of the countryside, and it is not surprising that the early Siamese who discovered the cave decided to use it as a temple.

COUNTRY ROAD: BAREFOOT TRAFFIC

THE dusty roads of Thailand pass through the low, flat rice fields of the south and central sections of the country. There are a few paved highways near the larger cities, but for the most part Thai roads are better for walking than for motoring. An occasional bus or truck rattles past, leaving a choking cloud of dust in its wake. In the rainy season this sandy road will become a river of mud, and many a motorist will sink to his hubcaps long before reaching his destination.

None of these problems concern the Thai villagers. They walk, as the women are doing here, in as much comfort as possible. An umbrella is important in this country of brutal sunlight, and each woman moves in her own little pool of shade. Clothing is at a minimum—shoes are seldom worn, and the rest of the women's dress is simplicity itself. A length of cotton or silk, called a *pasin* (*pah-sin*), is wrapped around the waist like a skirt, and a fresh white blouse completes the costume. Men and boys wear even less. A twist of cloth around the hips, another about the head, and a country man is in the middle of his wardrobe. These people —men, women and children—can spend long hours in the rice fields, from which they walk home carrying loaded baskets. The trick is that no one talks about the weather—they do something about it instead.

Ricksha drivers catch a nap in the rare moments when their vehicles are not in demand.

62

RICE FARMERS: PRECIOUS CROP

THE wealth of Thailand springs each year from these tender green fields of rice. Most of the people are farmers, and much of the arable land is planted in one crop—rice. Although the planting and cultivating is tedious work, the Thais count themselves lucky. Their fields yield more than enough food for their own needs, and much of the rice is exported to feed their hungry Asiatic neighbors. As a result, Thailand has an economic independence that gives the nation unique power in its part of the world.

Most farmers own their own land, and the entire family works during the rice season. The fields are flooded with water pumped from the canals, and the primitive irrigation devices are usually some form of treadmill and paddle on which father and sons spend weary hours. The transplanting of the seedlings is frequently done by women, while the men plow the muddy fields with the help of a water buffalo. Later, when the rice begins to ripen, children stand guard over it with slingshots, making lively and effective scarecrows.

At harvest time, reaping becomes a gay community affair in which neighboring farmers help one another to bring in their crops. Each family sells its surplus rice to the government, and the family's supply for the coming year is stored in tall baskets kept safely under the house. The full rice baskets represent a real basic security. The Thais ask for little more than this, and they work just enough to eat, to enjoy a few simple pleasures, and above all to get the most *sanuk* (*sah*-NOOK), or joyousness, out of life. As a result their country seems, by Western standards, to be underdeveloped and the people lacking in ambition. But the Thais' accomplishments can best be measured by the beautiful things they have created and the happy lives they lead.

RUINS AT
LOP BURI:
ANCIENT
CAPITAL

THE good life can be traced far back to the earliest days of Siam. Six hundred years ago, one of the first kings had his state-of-the-nation report inscribed on stone, and it said in part, "This kingdom of Sukhothai is good: in the water there are fish, in the fields there is rice. The king does not levy taxes." That is a blueprint for a happy land in any age, and it is remarkable that the same words are true of Thailand today. The country has gone on from century to century, changing very little, and leaving only meager records of its history. Those records, for the most part, are the ruins of dead cities—the once-splendid capitals of the past.

We are looking at the moldering remains of the old capital of Lop Buri (*lohp boo*-REE). The fine buildings are shabby and broken, the stone Buddha—once dazzlingly gilded—now bears only a few faint smudges of gold. But the rich life in this fertile land has pushed up between the bricks, and the bright green of jungle and field spreads through deserted courtyards. Cities may come and go, but the fruitful earth endures.

Lop Buri today is a garrison town some 70 miles to the north of Bangkok. At one time, long before the Thais moved their kingdom so far south, this was the capital of Cambodia. In the seventeenth century, when Ayudhya was the Siamese capital, the king established another capital here, to serve as a summer residence and also as a second line of defense, should Ayudhya fall to the Burmese enemy. We can still see parts of his palace and the enormous royal elephant stables which remind us that in those days the Siamese cavalry numbered several thousand elephants. The remains of an ancient Cambodian wat with three pagodas loom over the present town, and from it and the ruined palace, historians must try to piece together the fragments of Siamese history. This is a country where the written word has assumed importance only in the past hundred years or so.

MASTER
AND PUPIL:
STUDY
IN REPOSE

FOLLOWING the example of Buddha, many of his disciples still sit under a tree and teach. Here, in the quiet shade, an older monk and a novice are seen in the classic posture of Buddhist contemplation. In the thousands of wats scattered all over Thailand, young men come not only to learn doctrine; frequently they are taught to read and write by the monks. The wats have for centuries been the only schools where Thai children could receive a formal education. Even now, when primary school education is compulsory, 40 per cent of the schools are in wats.

Until fairly recent times, knowledge was handed down from parents to children, and while the Thais had a rich store of racial wisdom, book learning was unknown to most of them. Practical skills, folklore and a wealth of amusing proverbs, for which the Thais have a particular fondness, still make up the backbone of their education. Children are brought up on sayings like, "When the water comes up, the fish will eat the ants, but when the water subsides it will be the turn of the ants to eat the fish." Another adage teaches, "If you want to choose an elephant, base your choice on its tail, but if you want to choose a girl, check up on her mother." Equipped with this home-taught approach to life's realities, the people of Thailand meet their problems with smiling equanimity.

Schools are in temples, and the school bus is a boat paddled along the canals.

ELEPHANTS AT WORK: NORTHERN TEAK FORESTS

LITTLE elephants begin to learn their trade from big elephants, and without these highly skilled workers, Thailand's teak industry would be unable to function. Most of the northern part of the country is primitive jungle, and these great beasts have been trained to haul out the heavy timber and bring it to a river for transportation. The elephants move slowly and methodically about their tasks. Those with young calves keep the babies at their side, yet they never tread on them or bump them. The calves try to stay in the shade created by their mothers' large shadow, and though their maneuvers may be troublesome, the grown elephants are patient with them.

Each elephant has a driver, or *mahout* (*muh-*HOUT), and man and beast have usually grown up together, starting as playmates and learning to work as partners. This ensures that both members of the team will have a long, productive life together. An elephant panics easily when alone, but with his *mahout* riding on his neck the animal remains calm. The Thais, always handy with a proverb, say, "When the elephant has two hearts he is not afraid." *Mahouts* and elephants communicate in Burmese, the common language of pachyderms and their handlers in all parts of Asia. These educated beasts know exactly how to handle the teak logs which sometimes weigh several tons. They drag them to the riverbank, then kneel and nudge the log into the water with skillful movements of their trunk. If a log jam develops, the elephant himself figures out how to break it up by using his tusks or by lifting one of the pieces of teak until the rest of the wood is moving again.

An elephant will work only five hours a day, and it must have a bath and rubdown each evening or it becomes grouchy. People who have watched these animals at work say that they have a ponderous dignity, and an intelligence that is almost human. The plains and jungles of Thailand abound in an astonishing variety of wildlife, but the trained elephants of the teak forests are surely the kings of the Siamese beasts.

HILL TRIBE GIRLS: WILD BORDER COUNTRY

THE savage beauty of the hill country in northern Thailand is very different from the broad, rice-growing plain in the center of the country. Here teak forests cover the land, and giant trees, more than a thousand years old, blot out the sun. In the lush jungles, pythons and king cobras slither through tangles of greenery. The rivers are alive with sleepy crocodiles, while leopards and tigers stalk silently through the forests. No sensible Thai will even breathe the word "tiger" while in the jungle, for fear that one of the fierce creatures will leap out at him. Herds of wild elephants trample the upland plains, and thousands of monkeys chatter noisily in the trees.

In the wild forests, hill tribes live, following customs and ways of their own. These two girls look more Chinese than Thai, and their clothing—especially the skullcaps—owes much to the Chinese fashion. There is no telling what is in the basket carried on the back of the little mountain pony but it may be opium. The remote hill people cultivate the opium poppy on their secluded slopes, and Bangkok has long been one of the world's chief sources for illegal opium—although use of the drug in Thailand is not against the law. The Thais also have a good-natured tolerance for the other peoples within their borders, and Chinese, Malayans, Europeans and these hill tribesmen are all permitted to live as they choose.

The opium poppy, source of medicines and escapist dreams, grows in the northern hills.

TEAKWOOD CARVER: CRAFTSMAN OF CHIANG MAI

ALTHOUGH the northern part of Thailand is largely primitive and underdeveloped, many of Siam's oldest cities, remnants of ancient tribal states, are found here. Chief among them is Chiang Mai (*chee*-AHNG MY), the second largest city in Thailand. Its age-old walls can no longer contain this thriving center of the teak industry, and exotic merchants from China and Burma do an active business here with Thai traders. Chiang Mai can also boast some of the best craftsmen in all of Thailand, whose skill at silk and cotton weaving, pottery, silverware and teak carving is bringing the old city new fame.

This artist has re-created one of the favorite stories of Thai history in his teakwood statue. The tide of conquest between Siam and neighboring Burma surged back and forth for many centuries, and its most colorful episode is known as "The War of the Seven White Elephants," an event which took place 400 years ago. In those days the rare white elephant (really an albino with a blotchy pink-and-gray coloring) was considered sacred and lucky, and could belong only to the king. Siam's king had the good fortune to possess seven of these fabulous beasts, while the king of Burma had none. The Burmese monarch requested a fairer redistribution of lucky elephants, and he was firmly refused. Thereupon he marched into Siam at the head of a large army and besieged the capital of Ayudhya.

The king of Siam, Maha Chakrapat (*mah*-HAH *chahk-krah*-PAHT), rode out to battle sitting on the neck of his elephant, and he and the Burmese king, mounted on a plain gray elephant, engaged in hand-to-hand combat. The Siamese queen Suriyothai (*soo*-REE-*yoh*-TIE) disguised herself as a warrior so that she could accompany her lord. When he was about to receive a mortal blow, the queen threw herself in front of him and was killed instead. She has been one of the favorite national heroines ever since, and her deed has been depicted by Thai artists in every craft.

74

THEATRICAL PROPS: REGAL SPLENDOR

THE Thai genius for decoration blossoms in numberless crafts, but it comes to full flower in their brilliant theater. Plays are acted on a stage as bare and simple as that of the Greek drama. A few potted plants indicate a forest or garden, a bench and a screen are the only furniture. But simplicity stops there. The players on this unadorned stage wear costumes that are strikingly magnificent—they exaggerate the splendor of ancient Siamese royalty. And topping off the costumes, many of the actors wear towering masks, carved and brightly painted like the demon mask seen here.

Another popular form of Thai drama is the marionette show. The little figures are operated by strings pulled from below. Their costumes are as richly designed as those of the human actors, and they are such works of art that some of the wonderful old figurines have been preserved in the National Museum. The marionettes move through the action of a play while a singer chants the story, accompanied by a chorus and musicians. Modern Thai audiences come to the theater to be amused, so the more serious ancient dramas have given way to versions in which clownish characters play an important part. The dialogue is peppered with jokes, and the marionettes cut amusing capers while the off-stage narrator fills in the funny lines.

A modern microphone carries the words of old Siamese drama to enchanted listeners.

77

TEMPLE MUSIC: MELODIES TO REMEMBER

THE gay and exotic charm of this country is compounded of its sights and sounds—the cheerful people, the jungle creatures that still lurk in its forests, the magic of its old temples. Here in the center of Lop Buri a shrine has been built high on a huge rock. Swarms of playful monkeys caper outside, and you can hear their shrill chatter above the sweet sounds of the temple music—reminding you that much of this land is still untamed. Inside, the wind blows through the open walls, setting the decorations dancing. On the floor, musicians play ancient instruments of bamboo, the old tunes strange and haunting, preserved only in the memories of each generation.

On a platform in front of the gilded images, bowls filled with burning joss sticks give the air a pungent scent. Masks of leopards and tigers hang on the wall, and when the monkeys outside grow too bold, a temple attendant takes one of the masks and shakes it threateningly at the frisky creatures. Then they skitter away from the rock and leap for the nearby trees, where their scolding can be heard in the highest branches.

People wander in and out, bringing fresh flowers, lighting joss sticks, rattling a bamboo container filled with numbered sticks until one stick falls out. A priest takes the stick and gives the person a slip of paper in return. The paper has a fortune written on it, and sometimes when the fortune is especially good, peals of laughter join with the sounds of music.

In front of the temple a man stands surrounded by caged birds that flutter in their little wicker cells. For a few cents people can buy one and set it free, thus acquiring merit. As the bird wings off into the sky, high above the flashing temple spires, it seems to be a symbol of the blithe, free spirit of Thailand.

SOME FAMOUS NAMES IN THAI HISTORY

KUBLAI KHAN (1216-1294)—*Mongol conqueror of China. His conquest drove Thais southward into Chao Phraya valley.*

RAMA KAMHENG (reigned 1275-1317)—*Greatest ruler of Sukothai period. Military and cultural leader. Introduced Cambodian alphabet to Siam.*

U-THONG (14th century)—*Moved capital south to Ayudhya, where it remained for 417 years.*

MAHA CHAKRAPAT (16th century)—*Ruler of Siam at time of War of the White Elephants (1548) with Burma. His queen, Suriyothai, sacrificed her life in battle to save her husband's.*

CONSTANTINE PHAULKON (17th century)—*Greek who became Prime Minister of Siam, and as powerful as the king. Encouraged French influence in the country.*

GENERAL TAKSIN (18th century)—*Part-Chinese general who drove Burmese invaders from Siam. Became king with capital at Thonburi. Executed when he went mad.*

GENERAL CHAKKRI (reigned 1782-1809)—*As Rama I, started present dynasty with capital at Bangkok.*

RAMA IV (Mongkut) (reigned 1851-1868)—*Hero of* The King and I. *After 26 years in monastery became first modern ruler of Siam.*

ANNA LEONOWENS (1834-1914)—*English governess who started first school in Bangkok.*

RAMA V (Chulalongkorn) (1853-1910)—*Pupil of Anna Leonowens. Greatest modern king of Siam. His queen, Saovabha, started first girls' school, was patron of Red Cross and many other philanthropies.*

SUNTHORN BHU (19th century)—*One of Siam's greatest writers. Author of epic romance* Phra Apai.

RAMA VI (Vajiravudh) (1881-1925)—*King who was famous literary figure. Translated Shakespeare into Siamese; wrote plays, poems, essays and founded influential literary club.*

RAMA VII (Prajadhipok) (1893-1941)—*Seventy-sixth child of Chulalongkorn. Abdicated three years after 1932 coup d'état by Army, Navy and civilian leaders, organized as "The People's Party."*

PIBUL SONGGRAM (1897-   )—*Early leader of "People's Party." Prime Minister at the time of Japanese occupation of Thailand and from 1947 to 1957.*

PRIDI PANOMYONG (1900-   )—*Important government leader from time of 1932 coup. Now in exile in Red China.*

RAMA VIII (Ananda Mahidol) (1925-1946)—*Succeeded to throne at age of ten; died under mysterious circumstances.*

SARIT THANARAT (1900-1963)*Commander-in-Chief of Thai Army. Headed government since 1958.*

RAMA IX (Phumiphon Aduldet) (1927-   )—*Only king ever born in the United States. He and Queen Sirikit made a State Visit to President Eisenhower in 1960.*

THANOM KITTIKACHORN—*Prime Minister since 1963*

SOME IMPORTANT DATES IN THAI HISTORY

c. 650 A.D.   *Thai tribes organize into independent kingdom of Nanchao in southern China.*

c. 1250   *Mass migration of Thais southward due to Mongol conquest of China and Nanchao under Kublai Khan.*

c. 1260-1350   *Thais found kingdom of Sukothai in what is now northern Thailand.*

c. 1283   *Siamese alphabet borrowed from Khmers in Cambodia by King Rama Kamheng.*

1350   *King U-Thong founds new dynasty and establishes southern capital at Ayudhya.*

1511   *First European contact occurs when Portuguese are permitted to trade with Thais.*

1548   *War of White Elephants with Burmese king.*

1664   *Dutch gain a monopoly of Siamese trade. French intrigue for trading rights leads in 1688 to a popular revolt and prolonged civil war.*

1767   *Ayudhya falls to Burmese invaders; city is destroyed.*

1775   *General Taksin drives out Burmese invaders and founds new capital at Thonburi on west bank of Chao Phraya River.*

1782   *General Chakkri becomes King Rama I, founds present dynasty, and establishes capital at Bangkok, across the river from Thonburi.*

1824-1851   *Rama III reigns. Negotiates commerce treaty with Great Britain; treaty with U. S. follows in 1833.*

1851-1868   *Reign of Rama IV (Mongkut), characterized by closer relations with the West. Anna Leonowens starts first English school in Bangkok.*

1868-1910   *Rama V (Chulalongkorn), greatest modern Siamese king, abolishes slavery, sends ambassadors to European countries.*

1917   *Siam enters World War I on side of Allies.*

1920   *Siam becomes a member of League of Nations.*

1932   *Establishment of constitutional monarchy results from uprising of People's Party.*

1939   *Government changes name of Siam to Thailand. (Between 1946 and 1949 it was again called Siam, but is now officially Thailand.)*

1942   *Thailand is forced by Japan to declare war on Great Britain and the U.S. Free Thai resistance movement set up.*

1946   *After World War II ends, Thailand joins the United Nations.*

1953   *Thailand is first Asian nation to send troops to Korea to fight under U. N. flag.*

1954   *Thailand joins SEATO.*

1958   *Field Marshal Sarit Thanarat dissolves parliament, draws up new constitution, assumes power and leadership of government.*

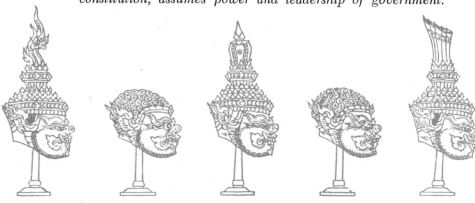

SOME THAI WORDS AND PHRASES

Here is a list of Thai words and phrases which would be useful for any visitor to Thailand. The pronunciation is given in simple phonetics, with the accented syllable in small capitals.

Do you speak English?
Tan pud pah-sah angkrit dai mai
(*tahn pood pah-sah ahng-*KREET *die my*)

How do you say . . . ?
Kam wah . . . pah-sah thai wah yang kai
(*kahm vah . . . pah-sah tie vah yahng kigh*)

Can you help me?
Tan tchuai lua chan noi dai mai
(*tahn tchoo-*EYE *loo-ah chahn noy die my*)

I don't understand.
Tschan mai kao chai (*chahn my cow chigh*)

What do you want?
Tan tong karn a-rai (*tahn tohng kahn ah-*RYE)

Please.
Dai prod (*die prohd*)

Thank you.
Kohb chai (*kohp chigh*)

Excuse me.
Kor tod (*koh tohd*)

It doesn't matter.
Mai pen rai (*my pen rye*)

Hello.   Goodbye.
Swasdi (*sah-vaht-*DEE) (*means both*)

Come here.
Chern kow mah dai (*churn cow mah die*)

Where is . . . ?
. . . you ti nai (*. . . you tee nigh*)

How much does it cost?
Rah kah tao rai (*rah kah tah-oh rye*)

Airport
sa-nahm bin (*sah-*NAHM *bin*)

Boat (ship)
ruah (ROO-*ah*)

Train
rod fai (*road fie*)

Airplane
ruah bin (ROO-*ah bin*)

Room
hong (*hohn*)

Food
ah-harn (*ah-hahn*)

Breakfast
ah-harn chao (*ah-hahn chow*)

Dinner
ah-harn kam (*ah-hahn kahm*)

Water
nam (*nahm*)

NUMBERS

One	nueng	(*nung*)
Two	song	(*sohng*)
Three	sahm	(*sahm*)
Four	si	(*see*)
Five	hah	(*hah*)
Six	hok	(*hohk*)
Seven	ched	(*chehd*)
Eight	pad	(*pahd*)
Nine	kao	(KAH-*oh*)
Ten	sib	(*seeb*)
One hundred	nueng roy	
	(*nung roy*)	
One thousand	nueng pan	
	(*nung pahn*)	

DAYS OF THE WEEK

Sunday	wan ah tit	(*vahn ah tit*)
Monday	wan chan	(*vahn chahn*)
Tuesday	wan ang-karn	(*vahn ahng-kahn*)
Wednesday	wan put	(*vahn poot*)
Thursday	wan paruhut	(*vahn pah-roo-*HOOT)
Friday	wan suk	(*vahn sook*)
Saturday	wan sao	(*vahn* SAH-*oh*)
Day	klang wan	(*klahng vahn*)
Night	klang kuen	(*klahng koon*)
Yesterday	muah wan ni	(*moo-ah vahn nee*)
Today	wan ni	(*vahn nee*)
Tomorrow	prung ni	(*proon nee*)
Tonight	kuen ni	(*koon nee*)
Week	sap-pa-dah	(*sap-pah-*DAH)

MONEY

baht (*baht*) or tical (TEE-*kohl*)

INDEX